IMPERIAL
ROME

IMPERIAL ROME

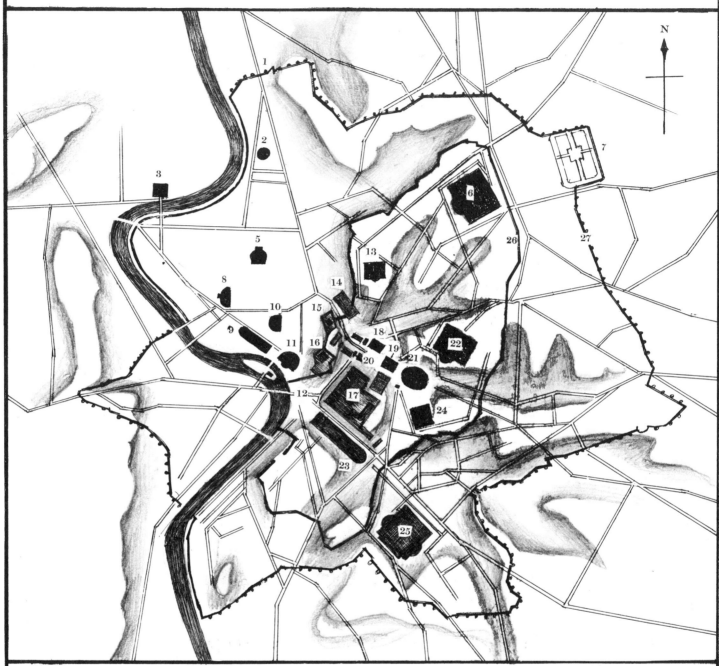

1. Porta Flaminia
2. Tomb of Augustus
3. Tomb of Hadrian
4. Basilica of St. Peter
5. Pantheon
6. Baths of Diocletian
7. Praetorian Camp

8. Theatre of Pompey
9. Circus Flaminius
10. Theatre of Balbus
11. Theatre of Marcellus
12. Forum Boarium
13. Thermae of Constantine
14. Forum of Trajan

15. Arx
16. Capitol
17. Palatine
18. Basilica of Constantine
19. Temple of Venus and Roma
20. Roman Forum

21. Colosseum
22. Thermae of Titus
23. Circus Maximus
24. Temple of Claudius
25. Baths of Caracalla
26. Servian Wall
27. Aurelian Wall

Scale ⊢———— ¼ ½ ¾ ————⊣ 1 Mile

IN THE AGE OF CONSTANTINE

IMPERIAL ROME

DRAWINGS BY ALAN SORRELL

TEXT BY ANTHONY BIRLEY

LUTTERWORTH PRESS · LONDON

First Published 1970

ACKNOWLEDGEMENTS

Alan Sorrell wishes to acknowledge, with grateful thanks, the help given to him by Professor D. E. Strong and Mr. Mark Hassall, of the Institute of Archaeology, London University.

The photographs of the Aurelian Wall (page 8), the Forum (page 17), and the Circus Maximus (page 40) are the copyright of Fototeca Unione, Rome. The Colosseum (page 11), and Trajan's Column (page 33), are by Foto-Enit-Rome, by courtesy of the Italian Tourist Office, London. The Roman street (page 26) is by Engelbert Reineke, of 693 Eberbach, Neckarhälde 26. The photographs of Castel Sant' Angelo (page 53), and of St. Peter's (page 43), are the copyright of A. F. Kersting.

ISBN 0 7188 1367 7

Printed in Great Britain
by Fletcher and Son Ltd, Norwich

ROME in A.D. 330 has reached a turning-point in her history. In this year the emperor is founding the new capital that bears his name, Constantinople. Rome's days as mistress of the world are over. Yet Constantine has already ensured that Rome will acquire a new pre-eminence, as the seat of the heir of St. Peter. His action in founding a New Rome on the Bosphorus is only the logical conclusion to a gradual process. During long decades his predecessors deserted Rome in favour of more strategically placed centres such as Milan, Trier and Niciomedia. The last emperor to rule from Rome was the usurper Maxentius, whom Constantine defeated at the battle of the Milvian Bridge in A.D. 312.

The traveller approaching Rome from the north follows the route that the victorious army took, down the via Flaminia. At Saxa Rubra he passes the place where Constantine in his tent saw the mystic sign that was to give him victory. Soon the city itself will be visible. When one crosses the Milvian Bridge one sees the mighty walls. Rome had had no physical defences for more than five centuries. Then, two generations ago, Aurelian judged the danger from northern invaders to be too serious. He constructed a wall some 26 feet high and 12 feet wide, with gates and towers, 12 miles in its total circuit. Forty years after this, Maxentius in preparation for a siege by Constantine strengthened these defences. But in the event he marched out to give battle and they were never put to the test.

The traveller coming to Rome for the first time, even with the knowledge that Constantinople is being founded as a rival, cannot fail to feel some strong emotion. For if a free man, living anywhere within the vast boundaries of the empire, that stretch from the Irish Sea to the Tigris and from the Danube to the Sahara, he is himself a Roman, a citizen of Rome. It is not mere chance that the foundation legend of the city recalls an outcast, suckled by a wolf, who took in other outcasts to people his new settlement. For Rome has indeed practised this policy. When through conquest she had transmitted the ancient civilization of the Mediterranean to the barbarous tribes beyond, in the north and west, she took them to herself. They became fellow-citizens.

It will be best to look at Rome from the south. This is the direction from which Romulus first saw it, according to legend, coming from Alba Longa. Romulus's city was merely a collection of thatched huts on the Palatine, the original Roma Quadrata, "four-square Rome". What was to become the Forum was then a marsh, giving protection to

The Flaminian Gate, one of the original gateways of the Aurelian Wall, built by Aurelian (A.D. 270–275).
In its circuit of 12 miles there were 16 gates and 383 towers, some of which are shown above, right.

the tiny settlement on its north-east side. By stages this village was extended north and east, taking in part of the Caelian and Esquiline hills. This became the "city of four regions" with the inclusion of the rest of the Caelian, the Viminal and Quirinal hills, and the sacred hill of Jupiter, the Capitol.

The earliest walls of the city are attributed to the sixth century B.C. king Servius Tullius. But the "Servian" Wall was in fact built after the Gauls captured Rome in 390 B.C. Its surviving stretches enclose an area vastly greater than the "city of four regions". On the south-west it flanks the Tiber. To the south it includes the Aventine hill, the trading quarter. On the west it runs past the Capitol, including within its circuit the place where the Baths of Constantine now stand, coming up as far as Diocletian's Baths, then turning south. Even if Servius Tullius did not build this wall, he and the Tarquins, the last three kings—all of them Etruscan—certainly transformed Rome. Under their rule it became a city as large and as splendid as many in Greece and most in Italy. The choice of site has been much admired. Italy after all has a central position in the Mediterranean, and

A section of the Aurelian Wall. An earlier line of fortifications which enclosed the "city of four regions" is said to have been built in the sixth century B.C., but the section of wall now seen by visitors near the Terminus Station was part of the "Servian Wall", which was built after the Gauls captured Rome in 390 B.C. The lines of the Servian and Aurelian Walls are shown on the key drawing, page 2.

Rome is centrally placed within Italy. Her river is the largest south of the Po, and it is navigable below the city. When Rome was founded, the rocky slopes of the Capitol, the Tiber and the marshes made it nearly impregnable. But the same features made it an unhealthy place to live—dangerous too, for the river floods frequently. The Etruscan kings drained the marshes and created the Forum. At the same time they created a sewerage system far in advance of anything of its kind elsewhere. The Cloaca Maxima still flows into the Tiber to witness to their engineering skill, when the architectural and artistic glories of Etruscan Rome have long disappeared.

After the destruction in 390 B.C. hasty rebuilding perhaps created the lack of order in the city's lay-out. Ironically Rome, that has imposed chess-board pattern street planning all over her empire, herself has very few long, straight streets, let alone a systematic town-plan. Even after defeating Hannibal the city looked undistinguished. The Forum contained few public buildings apart from temples and the senate-house (Curia). It was still not much more than a market-place. Nor were there any aristocratic mansions to lend dignity to the other parts of the city. In the second century B.C., when Rome became mistress of the Mediterranean, signs of her greatness at last appeared in the buildings of the city. Great halls (Basilicae) were put up in the Forum, temples were rebuilt on a grander scale and adorned with works of art, the booty of Sicily, Greece and the east.

In the first century B.C. Roman expansion really became imperialist. The dictator Sulla, Pompey, Caesar and finally Augustus, and a host of lesser figures, vied in spending vast sums from the proceeds of their eastern and northern conquests on the embellishment of the capital. Augustus "found Rome a city of brick and left her a city of marble". In one year alone (28 B.C.) he restored eighty-two temples. He repaired the Capitol and Pompey's theatre (the first stone theatre in Rome), the senate-house and countless other buildings. His new constructions include the Theatre of Marcellus, the new Fora named after himself and Caesar, the Temple of Apollo on the Palatine and the Temple of Mars Ultor (the Avenger). More important, perhaps, he and his lieutenant Agrippa, the builder of the Pantheon, gave real attention to public utilities—aqueducts, sewers, roads and bridges. Meanwhile those who had benefited from following Augustus were able to build themselves great mansions or palaces. The city had by now expanded to include the Campus Martius and further areas on east and south. But the slums of old Rome remained.

For fifty years after Augustus's death few changes were made. Tiberius increased the imperial residence on the Palatine. Claudius added various monuments. Then in A.D. 64 came the great fire. Ten out of the fourteen districts into which Augustus had divided the city were gutted. Nero took the opportunity. The city was replanned, with wider streets. A new building material was introduced, brick-faced concrete. This is far more fireproof than the travertine stone of the Augustan city, which crumbles badly under intense heat. A building boom was created which continued for more than half a century. Then it was reactivated, when it might otherwise have petered out, by the influx of riches from Trajan's conquests and the architectural enthusiasm of Hadrian. The family that owned most of the brickworks naturally made immense profits. With the accession of Antoninus Pius in A.D. 138 it supplied an emperor. At the end of the second century there was another serious fire (A.D. 191) which provided the opportunity for the extensive building operations of the Severan dynasty. The Baths of Caracalla are the most striking example of this phase. Then for more than fifty years Rome was neglected—apart from Aurelian's wall-building—until Diocletian (A.D. 284–305) and Constantine once more began spending money there.

A visitor who has never been to Rome before will probably want to see the Forum and Palatine first. The Palatine is inaccessible to the private citizen, even when the emperor is not in residence. But a walk from the lowest bridge over the Tiber, the pons Probi, will allow him to approach the Forum past the southern side of the Palatine. Then from the Forum, and later from the Circus Maximus, he will be able to see much of the palace. This route will also take the visitor through the commercial area, where essential shopping can be done. In this part of Rome aqueducts dominate the scene, bringing in water in great arches that span the streets—the aqua Marcia and the aqua Appia. Traffic is banned from the city in hours of daylight, and the streets are crowded with pedestrians. Here and there some eminent or wealthy person is being carried in a litter. On the ground floor, at street level, the shops display their wares, often putting them out on the pavements. Above street level the blocks soar upwards, many exceeding the height limit of 60 feet that successive emperors have repeatedly enforced. The traveller may be disposed to order some new clothes, attracted by the advertisements of a draper's shop. But he will probably be horrified at the high prices—Diocletian's Edict on Maximum Retail Prices never worked and is now a dead letter.

The Palatine, that forms the Tenth Region of the city, is now entirely occupied by the palace, except for its lower slopes facing the Circus Maximus and on the south side opposite the Temple of Claudius. There shops and houses crowd the imperial residence. The grassy

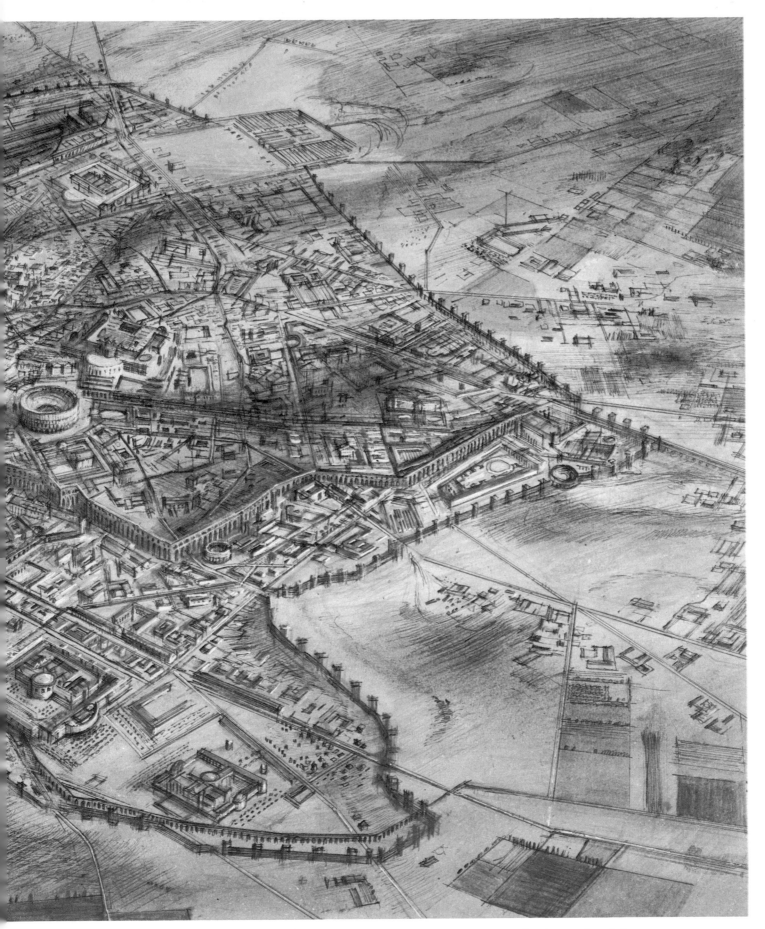

A panoramic view of the ancient city in about A.D. 330. *Note how the Aurelian Wall embraces the whole area, which includes a part on the west bank of the Tiber. The main buildings can be identified from the map on page 2.*

A street scene, showing the arch of an aqueduct carrying the city's water supply.

A typical open-fronted shop with customers and an attendant slave.

hill that Aeneas is supposed to have visited a millennium and a half ago was then occupied only by shepherds and their flocks. Whatever the truth of that legend, by 800 B.C. simple huts were built on its slopes by the first of a long series of occupiers. But in A.D. 330 the buildings that cluster thickly on the Palatine recall only the long line of emperors. Augustus was born in a private house on one corner of the hill in 63 B.C. By the time of his death in A.D. 14 he had made the whole of it his property. But the Palatine is associated above all with the gloomy reputation of Tiberius, his successor, of Domitian, the cold and hated emperor murdered there in A.D. 96, and of Severus, who seized Rome in A.D. 193. It was Severus who gave the complex of palaces its final form. The visitor passing on the southern side will notice a remarkable structure that he built, the Septizonium. Going past this, one sees soaring overhead the "Neronian arches" that carry the aqua Claudia into the palace. On the right is the grandiose Temple of Claudius, and ahead the newly erected Arch of Constantine, nearly 70 feet high. It was set up by the senate and people of Rome, who attribute Constantine's victory, in the inscription, to "the inspiration of divinity and the greatness of his mind".

After passing the Arch of Constantine the traveller may not know where to turn. To his right looms the great amphitheatre, ahead the grotesquely enormous Colossus, to his left the largest temple in the city, of Venus and Rome. Between this and the Temple of the Caesars stands the Arch of Titus, through which the Sacred Way (Sacra via) runs down into the Forum. The glittering series of white and gold buildings that can be glimpsed beyond it may dazzle a raw provincial. He may be inclined to rush on nervously, past the Colosseum and up the sloping road leading to the Baths of Titus, before turning to look back at the splendid scene.

The Palatine and surrounding buildings.

Rising up on the skyline, higher than anything, is the Temple of Juno Moneta on the Arx of the Capitol. Farther to the left, lower but more massive, is the shrine of the three protecting deities of Rome—Juno, Minerva and, above all, Jupiter Best and Greatest, after whom the Temple is named. Moving down the eye comes to the two-storied Tabularium, where the state records are housed, and then the Temple of Saturn, the ancient treasury of the Roman people. Nestling behind it is the Temple of Vespasian, to the right of the Temple of Concord. Beyond this, farther to the right, are the ill-omened Gemonian Steps, down which the bodies of enemies of the people used to be hurled, after execution

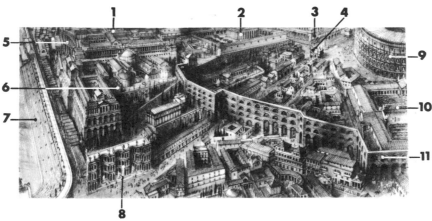

(1) *The Palatine.* (2) *Temple of the Caesars.* (3) *Temple of Venus and Roma.* (4) *Arch of Constantine.* (5) *Palace of Augustus.* (6) *Palace of Septimius Severus.* (7) *Circus Maximus.* (8) *Septizonium.* (9) *Colosseum.* (10) *Temple of Claudius.* (11) *Aqua Claudia.*

in the grim state prison (Tullianum) on the other side. The Arch of Severus now dominates this end of the Sacred Way, depriving the Rostra of the key position they once had. From here the politicians of the free Republic harangued the assembly. Here the revolutionary tribunes Tiberius and Gaius Gracchus put their proposals to the sovereign plebs. Here Cicero roused the people against Catiline in 63 B.C. and attacked Antony twenty years later—and here the affronted Antony placed his enemy's head after his murder. Facing the Comitia, where the assembly once met, is the Curia, destroyed by fire in A.D. 283 and recently rebuilt by Diocletian to its old design. Here the Roman Senate still meets. The old aristocracy has now disappeared, but there are still senators who can claim some tenuous links with the nobility of the late Republic and early Empire. These and others allied to them by marriage and mutual interest maintain with tenacity the show of ancient ceremony, secular and religious, which no longer has any meaning in political reality. Looking towards the left again, the Basilica Julia with its great arcades can be seen, and the space between it and the Basilica Aemilia opposite is crowded with statues and other monuments. Next to it is the Temple of Castor and Pollux, behind them the Temple of Augustus. This end of the Forum is almost made into an enclosed square by a group of smaller buildings nearer the observer—the little circular shrine of Vesta, the Regia and the Temple of Julius. In the foreground the Temple of Antoninus and Faustina looms up and closer still the Temple or Forum of Peace, and, beyond, the other imperial Fora.

After this long gaze from a distance, the time has come to enter the Forum. If the visitor makes a circuit round the east side he can come in by the Argiletum street and the Forum of Nerva or Forum Transitorium. He will pass the Curia on his right and the Basilica Aemilia on his left and will then be standing on the edge of the Sacred Way. The overwhelming impression is bound to be one of a crowded display of wonderful sights. Facing him is a row of seven columns crowned with statues, in front of the Basilica Julia, even more splendid than the Aemilian, which was the first to be built in Rome. In its present form the main hall of the Aemilia is nearly 300 feet long and nearly 90 feet wide, with white and coloured marble columns inside and red granite columns in its portico outside. The Julian Basilica occupies a space 330 feet long by 160 feet wide. It faces the Sacred Way, while its two short sides are bounded by the vicus Tuscus and the vicus Jugarius, ancient streets leading to the Forum Boarium and the Tiber. Its main hall is surrounded on all sides with two aisles, above which are the galleries of the upper storey, forming an open arcade. Inside the Basilica the law-courts used to meet, and outside it the bankers and financiers set up their stalls. Flanking the Basilica the eleven fluted white marble columns of the Temple of Castor face the onlooker. First dedicated in 484 B.C. this temple played a prominent part in public life, for the Senate used often to meet there. Between this temple and the Aemilian Basilica, facing the Rostra and the Capitol, stands the temple of the deified Julius. It was built by Augustus on the spot where Caesar's body had been burnt after his murder. In front of the temple is a platform with a round altar. Inside stands a colossal statue of the deified dictator, first of the Caesars, with a comet on

The Forum today, looking towards the Arch of Septimius Severus and the Temples of Saturn, Vespasian and Concord, and, beyond, the Tabularium. Compare this with the reconstruction drawing on the next page.

The Roman Forum, looking towards the Capitol.

(1) *Forum Boarium.* (2) *Janiculum.* (3) *Island.* (4) *Basilica Julia.* (5) *Capitol.* (6) *Temple of Jupiter Optimus Maximus.* (7) *Temple of Saturn.* (8) *Temple of Vespasian.* (9) *Tabularium.* (10) *Temple of Concord.* (11) *The Arx: Temple of Juno Moneta.* (12) *Temple of Augustus.* (13) *Temple of Castor and Pollux.* (14) *Lacus Juturnae.* (15) *Temple of Vesta.* (16) *Regia.* (17) *Arch of Augustus.* (18) *Temple of Julius Caesar.* (19) *Temple of Antoninus and Faustina.* (20) *Lacus Curtius.* (21) *Basilica Aemilia.* (22) *Rostra.* (23) *Arch of Septimius Severus.* (24) *Curia.* (25) *Forum of Nerva (Transitorium).* (26) *Forum of Julius Caesar.* (27) *Tullianum.*

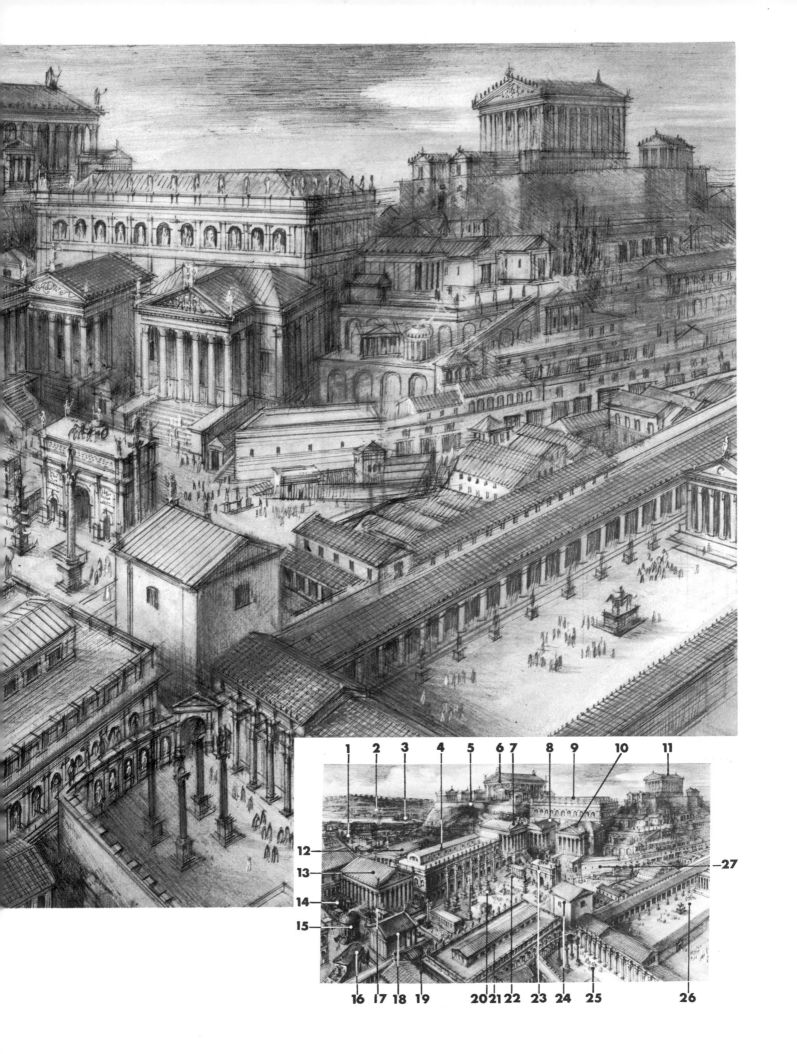

Looking from the Palatine towards the Colosseum.

the head. On the other side of the temple is a building shaped like an irregular pentagon. This is the Regia, the official headquarters of the Pontifex Maximus, built of blocks of white marble. Here the chief priest of the Roman state has to conduct meetings of the college of pontiffs, and keeps the archives of the city's religious and official year. Beside it is the circular shrine of Vesta, where the Vestal Virgins tend the sacred fire and other mysteries of the ancient Roman religion. The Vestals live in a special Atrium, connected by arches on its far side to buildings in front of the palace, across the Nova via.

20

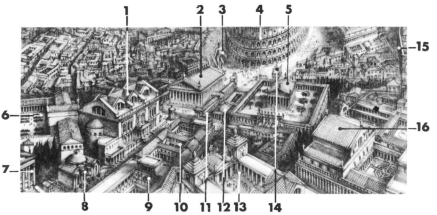

(1) *Basilica of Constantine.* (2) *Temple of Venus and Roma.* (3) *Sun God (Colossus).*
(4) *Colosseum.* (5) *Temple of the Caesars.* (6) *Temple of Peace.* (7) *Temple of Antoninus and Faustina.* (8) *Temple of Romulus.* (9) *House of the Vestals.* (10) *Granaries.* (11) *Arch of Titus.* (12) *Temple of Jupiter Stator.* (13) *Palace of Tiberius.* (14) *Arch of Constantine.* (15) *Aqua Claudia.* (16) *Imperial Palace.*

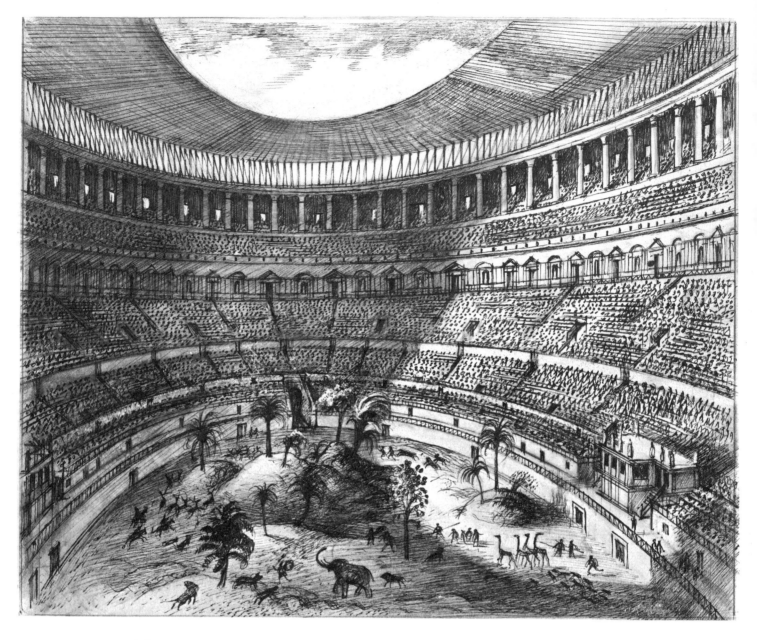

If the visitor can gain access to one of the apartment houses on the Nova via, by ascending to the roof he gains an excellent vantage point from which to inspect the most impressive new building in the Forum, the New Basilica, begun by Maxentius and completed by Constantine. This Basilica is more like the great halls in the public baths than the traditional long hall of the Julian and Aemilian Basilicae. It was originally designed to face east, with five entrances. Constantine made a new entrance, with fine porphyry columns, on the south side, to give access from the Sacra via. This enormous building blocked the existing road from the Baths of Titus to the Forum, for its north-west corner was built right up against the library of the Temple of Peace. Maxentius constructed an underground passage some 50 feet long to deal with this problem. Opposite the New Basilica, where the Sacred Way is at its widest, stand great granaries. They occupy the spot where Nero had erected the entrance-hall to his grandiose Golden House. The road is diverted

Left. *The Colosseum, also known as the Flavian Amphitheatre, in plan an ellipse measuring 620 feet by 513 feet, with seats for 50,000 spectators. In the arena were held gladiatorial and wild beast shows of extraordinary brutality and extravagance.*

at this point—it comes out through the Arch of Titus from the arched colonnade next to the Temple of Venus and Roma. This temple of two goddesses was built by Hadrian to his own design. Venus occupies the eastern half, facing the Colosseum, Roma faces west towards the Capitol. Maxentius restored it after damage by fire in 307, making it once more the most magnificent—or, at least, the largest—temple in the city. It is built of brick-faced concrete, with a marble veneer, and white marble columns. South of it stands the Arch of Titus, commemorating the destruction of a very different temple, that at Jerusalem, in A.D. 70. Beyond this is the little Temple of Jupiter Stator, then some blocks of apartment houses encroaching on the area between the palace and the Sacred Way.

Dominating the entire scene is the incredible bronze statue of the Sun God. A hundred feet high, standing on a concrete base 23 feet square, it is justly named the Colossus. The statue was at first given the features of Nero, but after his death the head was altered. Hadrian moved it to its present position next to the amphitheatre when constructing his new temple, and in time its proximity to the great arena was to give rise to the name Colosseum. The gigantic statue has become associated in men's minds with the fortunes of Rome: "As long as the Colossus stands, Rome too will stand. When the Colossus falls, Rome too will fall. When Rome falls, the world will fall." A visit to the Colosseum is an essential part of any visit to Rome, even if one is familiar with such places. For this is the largest of its kind in the world. It was built by the Flavian dynasty that took power

The Colosseum as it is today, ruined by earthquakes, and despoiled for building material. The floor of the arena has been destroyed, revealing the complicated substructures below.

after the fall of Nero. Entertainment for the people on this massive scale has been a vital means of retaining popularity for all emperors. At that time, since the site had been confiscated by Nero to form part of the pleasure-grounds of his Golden House, its transfer back to public use was of course a much appreciated gesture.

From its opening in A.D. 80 the place has been the scene of bloodshed on a horrifying scale. Now, 250 years later, gladiatorial combats are officially discouraged—for, after all, some of the blood that has stained the arena was shed by Christian martyrs. But Constantine is far away building his new Christian capital. Performances are no longer heavily subsidized by state patronage. But they still go on. For each show awnings are erected from massive poles. This tricky operation necessitates the permanent presence in the city of a detachment of the Italian fleet. Only regular sailors have the expertise required to handle the great expanses of canvas which protect those not in the shaded half from the glaring rays of the afternoon sun. Fifty thousand people can be squeezed in, separated from the arena itself and from one another by an intricate seating arrangement. The seats and rows are all numbered and access to each block is strictly controlled, through the numerous broad passageways (vomitoria). When men and animals are to be killed in front of a crowd of this size, very special care has to be taken.

After the performance the audience returns home. Those who have occupied the

A mansion and gardens on the Janiculum.

privileged front rows go to their stately mansions or palaces, on the Caelian or Pincian hills or across the Tiber on the Janiculum. There are nearly 1,800 of these mansions (Domus) in fourth-century Rome. Such houses as these are in extensive grounds, with formal gardens adorned with fountains, statues, flights of steps and covered walks, with trees and bushes to provide shade and colour. The houses themselves contain the great urban household (familia) of men whose possessions in many cases spread over half the Mediterranean world, sometimes beyond. The façades are of marble, and the rooms are so designed as to look in on a central court. The pagan aristocracy is haughty and self-contained, living a life quite unlike that of anyone else in the Empire. The proletariat returns to very different living conditions. Most of them live in slum tenements, in blocks six or more storeys high (insulae). Unlike those who live in the aristocratic

Shops and houses.

Tenements and slums in the ancient city. Right, *a similar scene in modern Rome.*

mansions, they have no piped water. Inside their homes the rooms are cramped and over-crowded, with little in the way of furniture. There are over 40,000 such blocks of tenements in Rome. Their inhabitants, hundreds of thousands of them, look on their homes merely as places to sleep and to keep any precious possessions they may have. In the circumstances people are naturally disposed to spend as much of their time as possible outside their houses, either at the theatre, amphitheatre or circus, or at the Baths. In this respect they are well off, for Rome has eleven great Public Baths.

Of these the Baths of Diocletian are undoubtedly the most attractive to someone who can pick and choose. They are not the most recent, for Constantine himself has only lately completed a new establishment on the Quirinal hill. But Diocletian's Baths, finished thirty years ago, are the most splendid in the city, and hence in the world. They are even more sumptuous than the Baths of Caracalla at the southern end of the city. They stand in the north-east corner of Rome, opposite the old parade-ground of the Praetorian Guard (now out of use, for Constantine disbanded the Guard in A.D. 312), on the other side of the Servian Wall. Three thousand people can be accommodated at one time, spread out among the various sections. Any provincial is accustomed to the pattern.

27

The vast baths of Diocletian spread over 27 acres. This drawing shows the Frigidarium—the cold swimming pool of the Baths.

After going from the changing-rooms (apodyterium) to the tepidarium with gentle heat, the caldarium or hot bath and the laconicum where the intense dry heat causes profuse sweating, the bather can finish with a dip in the magnificent open-air cold pool (frigidarium). Then, relaxed and refreshed—after ending up with a massage and perhaps a shave or hair-cut—one can stroll up and down in the concourse in the great hall. One can observe one's fellow-bathers of all types, the grand accompanied by their slaves carrying their clothes. If one is tempted, there is ample choice for a snack, with sausagemen, cakesellers and confectioners of all kinds crying their wares. After this it will be time to stumble home through the packed streets. If night has fallen it may well be necessary to

The Baths of Diocletian; The Great Hall. It fell into disrepair over the centuries, but in the 1500s Michelangelo converted the Hall into a church which was called Santa Maria delgi Angeli. It was much altered in 1749.

enlist the aid of friends, and perhaps a hired torchbearer, to fight one's way through the chaotic mass of wheeled vehicles that have now been let into the city.

The visitor may have seen the Capitol already from the Forum and have ascended to the Arx by the Gemonian Steps or the winding Clivus Argentarius or the steep Sacred Way itself. But he must view it from another side, where the hundred steps go up to the Tarpeian Rock. Every Roman schoolboy knows the story of the traitress in the days of Romulus who let in the Sabines and was repaid with death. In truth the hill was not used at all at that time. It was the Tarquins, the Etruscan kings, who built the great temples there. Probably it was an Etruscan word associated with their name that caused first the whole hilltop and then just its steepest part to be called Tarpeian. The legend of the faithless Tarpeia was a subsequent invention, to account for the rock's grim use in later years. It is the place from which parricides and similar criminals are cast down to their death. The great Temple of Jupiter was begun by Tarquin I and continued by Tarquin the Proud. But—tradition states—it was only completed and dedicated after the expulsion of the king, by one of the first consuls of the new Republic, Horatius, in 509 B.C. This temple survived for 426 years until it was burned down in civil war in 83 B.C. Rebuilding was completed in 69 B.C., and the restored temple was likewise destroyed by fire in another civil war, in A.D. 69, the "year of the four emperors". The third temple survived a mere five years from its completion in A.D. 75. The fourth, the work of the extravagant Domitian, still stands in A.D. 330, retaining its claim to be regarded as the finest building in the world. Its "spacious columned halls", with pillars of gleaming white Pentelic marble, "its statues that seem to breathe" and its high-pitched roof covered with gilded bronze, have made it a fitting place for the most solemn ceremonies of the Roman commonwealth.

Foremost among these ceremonies is the triumph. The victorious generals of the Republic and then the conquering emperors have always ended their spectacular parade through the streets of Rome by giving thanks to the great god of Rome, who in Virgil's words has given the Romans "empire without end". Here the grim generals of the early Republic triumphed again and again, over Latins, Etruscans, Samnites and other Italian peoples. Here Flamininus and Paullus triumphed over Macedonia, and on 29th and 30th September 61 B.C. Pompey triumphed over half the known world—"Asia, Pontus, Armenia, Paphlagonia, Cappadocia, Cilicia, Syria, the Scythians, the Jews, Albania, the pirates". Here Caesar triumphed for his victories in Gaul, and Augustus for Actium where he defeated Cleopatra, Claudius for the conquest of Britain, Titus and Vespasian for the defeat of the great Jewish rebellion and Trajan for the conquest of Dacia. Most bizarre of all was the occasion when Hadrian supervised the posthumous Parthian triumph of Trajan, conducting the effigy of the dead conqueror in triumph through the city, to lay the laurel of victory on the knees of Jupiter and give the sacrifice of thanksgiving.

Past triumphs are commemorated in solid form by the Arches of Claudius, Titus, Severus and other emperors, and, most remarkably of all, by the Columns of Trajan and Marcus Aurelius. The Column of Trajan must not be missed by any visitor. It is the first and still the most striking thing of its kind, and, besides, it is situated in Trajan's Forum, which may well be called "the supreme achievement of city-planning in Rome". The construction of this Forum completed the series of new imperial Fora, of Caesar Augustus, Vespasian and Nerva. These earlier Fora were designed as great squares with temples in the centre, so that the square forms the temple-courtyard. The temples are dedicated to Venus Genetrix, whom legend made the divine ancestress of the Julian house, Mars Ultor who enabled Augustus to take vengeance on Caesar's murderers, Peace, an appropriate enough deity for Vespasian, victor in the civil wars of A.D. 68–69, and Minerva, patroness of wisdom and favourite goddess of Domitian, the real builder of the

The Capitol, showing the Tarpeian Rock and the Temple of Jupiter Optimus Maximus.

Trajan's column and the Basilica Ulpia.

Forum named after his successor Nerva. The Forum of Trajan itself is an extensive open space, in the centre of which is a bronze equestrian statue of the emperor. The square is flanked on one side by a new hall opposite the Forum of Augustus, the Basilica Ulpia. Beyond the Basilica is the Temple of Trajan, in the forecourt of which stands the mighty Column, 128 Roman feet high. The other two sides of the Forum are hemicycles or half-circles. The left-hand side (as one enters the Forum from the Basilica), against the slope of the Quirinal hill, is the front of a new market, with large market-hall and shops going up in tiers. The whole Forum is colonnaded, and adorned with statues.

The architecture of the Basilica has so greatly impressed posterity that it is being used as a model by the architects of Christian churches. Trajan's monumental contribution to the transformation of Rome was marked symbolically by Hadrian. He placed an urn

Trajan's column today, hardly changed since the time it was built in A.D. 113, except that the statue of Trajan was replaced by that of St. Peter in 1587.

The Tomb of Hadrian, and (right, below) *as it is today, renamed Castel Sant' Angelo. It has had a very chequered history, being occupied as a fortress, a barracks, a prison, and is now a museum. It has been greatly altered over the centuries. The bridge, originally the Pons Aelius, is now known as the Ponte Santa Angelo.*

containing Trajan's ashes within the pedestal of the Column. This made Trajan the only man whose remains have legally been laid to rest within the Pomerium or sacred boundary of the city. All other burials have to be made outside (which is why the roads that lead to Rome are lined with funerary monuments). The Column, so strikingly situated, almost at the very centre of the city, and the most notable feature of the city's finest architectural complex, is a fitting symbol of what has made Rome great. Its very purpose seems to have been to mark the height of the ground excavated by Trajan's engineers to make room for the new market. This alone vividly attests the determination and the emphasis on achievement for practical, utilitarian ends, that has been contrasted by the Romans themselves with the useless magnificence of the Pyramids.

But the reliefs that decorate the Column depict in striking documentary fashion the working of thàt instrument that has carried Rome to world dominion, her army. The Column is in one sense a factual record of the two wars fought by Trajan against the Dacians. These led to the annexation of a vast new province in Transylvania (now abandoned to the Goths) and the capture of great quantities of gold, with the promise of more to come from the Transylvanian mines. The booty from these wars made possible Trajan's extensive programme of building. But the Column is more than a pictorial record of imperial victories. The visitor staring at the spiral reliefs, particularly if he can make use of the upper storeys of the Ulpian library for a close view of the details, will gain a deep impression of the incredible discipline and organization of the Roman army in the field. He will see it on the march, standards held high, weapons and kit smartly carried. He will see it building fortifications, each man knowing his own job, and the tented camps becoming miniature cities within a few hours. He will see the emperor conferring with his generals, inspecting his troops, and receiving the submission of the enemy; the legions and auxiliaries charging into battle; the artillery firing missiles; the field-surgeons at work dealing with the wounded; the signal-towers sending messages. This is the army that has gone to Scotland, to the Sahara, to Germany, to the Black Sea, Iraq and Egypt—"making a desert and calling it peace" in one view; but, in another view, making "a peace of immeasurable majesty". What Christian can doubt that the Roman soldiers, who built the roads that led from one quarter of the empire to another, have been instruments of divine Providence making possible the spread of the gospel?

The reign of Trajan was perhaps the high-water mark of Roman expansion. It is true that Severus added a further province, Mesopotamia, the northern part of the lands between the Euphrates and the Tigris. This conquest of the area fought over for so long between Rome and her eastern neighbours is celebrated by the Arch of Severus. But Hadrian abandoned far more extensive eastern conquests of Trajan, and Severus went only a small way towards redressing the balance. Hadrian began a policy of retrenchment and consolidation. Most important, he made Rome's frontiers in every part of the empire into something new and tangible, the fruits of his series of provincial tours. This achievement has made the name of Hadrian a familiar one to all who live in frontier provinces. Many

a visitor to Rome feels impelled to look for some visible record of Hadrian's activity in Rome itself. There is little that bears the emperor's own name, although he was a great builder. But he did leave one great and enduring monument to himself, his Mausoleum and the bridge that leads to it from the city, the pons Aelius. This recalls to Britons living near Hadrian's Wall the other bridge of that name that Hadrian built across the Tyne.

The Aelian bridge, with its lofty columns bearing statues, makes a splendid approach to the mighty tomb, which Hadrian began in A.D. 134. His ashes were placed there by his successor Antoninus in A.D. 139. The Mausoleum is in the Gardens of Domitia, on the right bank of the Tiber, a little downstream from the Mausoleum of Augustus, on the left bank in the Campus Martius. When Augustus died in A.D. 14 his Mausoleum already contained the ashes of numerous members of his tragic family—Marcellus his nephew and son-in-law, and his other son-in-law the great Agrippa, his grandsons Gaius and Lucius, his sister Octavia, his stepson Drusus. Augustus was followed by several of his successors and other members of the imperial family. Nerva's ashes were placed there in A.D. 98, but after that there was no more room. Trajan had his Column, but Hadrian needed a new tomb. The one he built is even more grandiose than that of Augustus. It is made of Parian marble, with a base 300 feet square. On this the circular Mausoleum itself is raised, some 200 feet in diameter and 70 feet high, surmounted by equestrian statues. The Antonine emperors that followed Hadrian made it their tomb as well, and the ashes of Severus, conveyed in an elaborate urn from York where he died in A.D. 211, were placed there by his sons Caracalla and Geta.

Hadrian and Severus both played a notable part in the restoration of the most remarkable building in this area of the city, the Pantheon, just over half a mile from the city end of the pons Aelius. Neither Hadrian nor Severus placed his own name on it, leaving intact the original inscription: "Marcus Agrippa, son of Lucius, three times consul, built this." Agrippa constructed the Pantheon as a shrine for the Julian family of his leader and father-in-law Augustus. It was only part of an architectural complex that included his Baths, the first in the city, and the Basilica of Neptune, built in tribute to the sea-god who had shown favour when Antony and Cleopatra were defeated at Actium. The shape of Agrippa's original Pantheon is now unknown. But few who know anything of the questing, inventive mind of Hadrian feel any doubt that it was he and his architects who were responsible for the dome and the rotunda, with its oculus (eye) at the top of the dome. "With its circular shape it resembles the vault of heaven," Cassius Dio commented in Severus's day. The seven niches hold statues of the seven planetary gods, and the oculus is the central and highest of seven concentric rings. The height is 140 feet from the floor to the oculus and it is 140 feet in diameter. This indicates that the superb symmetry of the shrine is grounded in deep religious—pagan—symbolism.

If the Pantheon was compared with the vault of heaven by the historian Dio, an anonymous poet has found that the Circus Maximus also deserves this description. The twelve-arched entry represents the twelve months, and the signs of the zodiac. The four

The Pantheon, considered to be the most perfect and best-preserved monument of Roman antiquity, though in mid-eighteenth century its interior was stripped of the Attic marble lining.

colours of the chariot-racing teams represent the four elements, and so on. A visitor who has been overawed by the number of spectators in the Colosseum will find the Circus even more alarming, for some 250,000 spectators can be accommodated here. Tradition credits the Etruscan kings with having converted the entire valley between the Palatine and the Aventine hills into this remarkable place of entertainment. But it was not until the times of Caesar and Augustus that this sports ground became anything more than a great open space with wooden stands for spectators around it; and it was Trajan who gave it its final form at the beginning of the second century A.D. By then, with the Colosseum devoted—since A.D. 81—exclusively to gladiatorial combats and similar spectacles, the Circus could be reserved principally for chariot-racing.

The four teams, Red, White, Green and Blue, compete round a track 600 yards long and 90 yards wide. To continue the elaborate cosmic simile of the poet, the course of the chariots round the circuits is compared with the passage of the sun round the heavens, with the metae at either end of the central spina marking as it were the rising and setting

The Circus Maximus, where chariot races took place before 250,000 spectators, was 2,000 feet long by 650 feet wide. The Imperial Box is shown in its favoured position opposite the end of the Spina which divided the arena longitudinally. The scene is dominated by the Palaces on the Palatine.

The Circus Maximus today.

of the sun. The canal that flows round the track, dividing it from the tiers of seats, is like the river of Ocean that surrounds the world. Seven laps constitute a circuit, just as the seven Zones bind the heavens together. Thus, the poet concludes, "our Circus performances harmonize with the divine order of the world: their great popularity increases to the honour of the gods". However this may be, the races are indeed enormously popular, and the charioteers are tremendous heroes. The racing stables are highly organized, with supporters' clubs, managers and the like, as well as the professional trainers, breeders and other necessary adjuncts of the racing world.

There is often keen competition to entice star charioteers to change their colours. One outstandingly successful performer, Gutta Calpurnianus, started his career with 102 victories for the Whites, transferred to the Reds, where he chalked up a further 78 successes, had his biggest run with the Blues, 583 first prizes, before the fourth faction, the Greens, finally secured his services, which brought 364 more winning performances. A magnificent tomb on the via Flaminia records the successes of Gutta in all their glory, with the names of his horses, Germinator and Niger, Afer and Silvanus, Nitidus and Saxo, and the rest. Seeing that over 170 days in the year are set aside for public holidays, with some form of public spectacle, Gutta and his fellows have always had plenty of work. Once the free Republic came to an end, the emperors realized only too well that the population of Rome, the descendants, in some degree at least, of the populus Romanus that had been the arbiter of power in the entire Mediterranean, must be diverted if it was not to become dangerously discontented. Not for nothing did Juvenal write that the people, "which once used to distribute power, the insignia of magistracy, the command over legions, everything, now restricts itself to two objects of anxious prayer, free bread and circus shows (panem et circenses)". The emperors have taken good care that this should be so. None the less, political displeasure voiced by hundreds of thousands of angry Romans in the Circus Maximus has caused the fall of more than one powerful minister and even emperor. The New Rome of Constantine on the Bosphorus is going to inherit this characteristic.

Whether he is a Christian or not, a visitor to Rome in the age of Constantine cannot fail to make a visit to one of the new wonders of the city, outside the walls on the right bank of the river. It is most easily reached by crossing the pons Neronianus, then turning left along the via Cornelia. One then goes past the Gardens of Agrippina, until, at the western end of the Campus Vaticanus one sees a great new building rising up, the Basilica of St. Peter. The apostle was buried in a Christian cemetery there after his martyrdom over 260 years ago. Now at last, there is an emperor who favours the Christian faith. He is not yet baptized, it is true—but it is normal practice to defer baptism until one's deathbed, so that the washing away of sins may be the more effective. The Christians can now come out into the open, out of their hidden underground places of worship. The magnificent church is being constructed with all the lavishness formerly spent on pagan temples and public buildings. Its design recalls not a temple but one of the assembly halls of the city.

Only if one is an initiate—and only men may be initiated—can one enter one of the shrines of Mithras, still, as always, hidden away from public gaze (not to escape persecution, although that day now seems likely to come, but to preserve the secrets of the mystic cult). Only just over twenty years ago the god Mithras reached the height of his popularity. The emperors met at the conference of Carnuntum on the Danube, and jointly dedicated an altar to "Mithras the Unconquered, Supporter of Our Rule". At that time the Church was licking its wounds after Diocletian's great persecution. The victory at the Milvian Bridge and the edict of toleration issued at Milan soon after, then finally Constantine's victory over Licinius in A.D. 323, have put the Christians in a position above all their rivals.

Leaving the Vatican, the visitor may like to stay for a while on the right bank to gaze at the Tiber, the river with which Rome's fortunes have been inextricably interwoven. Rome's rise to power in the first instance may plausibly be explained by her position. The city controls the lowest crossing of the Tiber. The fact that the river is sufficiently navigable for the dozen or so miles down to Ostia (the "mouths") allows the population to be supplied in relative safety, by barges. At the same time Rome is far enough away

41

The First Basilican Church of St. Peter built by Constantine on the site of the martyrdom of St. Peter in the Circus of Nero.

Right. *St. Peter's today, replacing Constantine's Basilica which was demolished in the early 16th century. Bramante and other architects developed the huge structure, and Michelangelo planned the great apses and the dome.*

Initiates worshipping at the shrine of Mithras.

from the coast to be immune to the menace of sea-raiders. In the middle of the river, opposite the Theatre of Marcellus, lies the little island. It is landscaped into the form of a ship, and joined to either shore by bridge, the pons Cestius and pons Fabricius. In the forward end of the "ship" is the Temple of Aesculapius, the god of healing, whose statue was brought to Rome from Epidaurus in Greece in 291 B.C. The delegation conducting the deity to his new home brought from Epidaurus a snake, thought to be the god himself in disguise. The snake went ashore on the island after wriggling away from its keeper, and there the temple was founded.

Farther downstream are the granaries and wharves, where the barges that supply the city are unloaded. For centuries Rome has depended on grain imported from overseas—Sicily, Egypt and Africa. Besides this basic commodity—and wine and oil—other products come in with an endless flow—spices, perfumes, jewels, wild beasts for the arena, cloth, timber, all the products of the Mediterranean and its hinterland. For the government this part of Rome is—together with the Circus Maximus and other places of entertainment—the object of its prime concern. Here the Statio Annonae is situated, where the corn to supply the dole is stored and distributed. The headquarters of the Annona is on the edge of the Forum Boarium, the principal meat-market of Rome. This market and the adjacent Forum Holitorium or vegetable market and the Velabrum district beyond supply the main needs of the city. The quadruple Arch has just been set up here, as a

The island in the Tiber, with the Circus Flaminius and the Theatre of Marcellus on the farther bank.

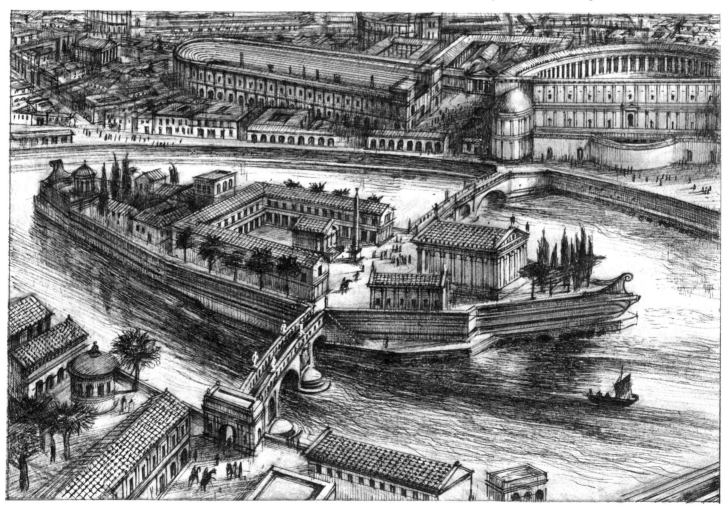

Granaries and wharves, with barges being unloaded.

meeting-place for bankers and the directors of the big companies that are involved in food wholesaling. It spans the street that leads from the Forum Boarium to the Velabrum.

The Forum Boarium is virtually an enclosed market, for it faces the river, and the twelve-arched gateway of the Circus Maximus is behind it (this is appropriate, for it means that the Circus and the Statio Annonae, the sources of Juvenal's *panem et circenses*, are only 90 yards from one another); while the old Servian Wall meets the Tiber at two points just above and just below the market. This area of the city is associated above all

45

The Forum Boarium seen from the Tiber, looking towards the Palatine.

with the name of Hercules. Tradition (enshrined in the Aeneid) asserts that he visited the site of Rome in the course of his labours, and killed the giant Cacus. The earliest shrine of the god in the city is here in the Forum Boarium, on the spot where he killed Cacus. It is a massive open-air altar, surrounded by a precinct wall, just outside the Circus starting-gates. Alongside this "Greatest Altar of Unconquered Hercules" is a circular temple of Hercules the Victorious. The onlooker from across the Tiber has his view of this blocked by another circular temple, dedicated to the ancient Italian god Portunus, protector of harbours. Close to the city side of the pons Aemilius, turning its back on the city, is the rectangular Temple of Mater Matuta, goddess of dawn, built in classical Ionic style.

46

The inquiring visitor who has seen something of how the capital's food supply arrives and is distributed may perhaps want to look more closely at its water-supply also. It is an attractive excursion to ride out of the city by the via Appia to see the aqueducts in open country. The Appian Way was first built, as a gravelled road, 631 years ago, but it has been paved along since, for miles south of Rome. Its course for the first few miles is lined with tombs, some of them grandiose marble monuments to distinguished individuals, some more modest affairs, and some communal vaults for whole families or for funeral clubs. Inside such tombs there are niches for the urns containing the ashes of each member of the family or club.

To gain the most striking view of the aqueducts the visitor is well advised to follow the Appian Way for a few miles. The same man that built this road was also responsible for the first of the eleven aqueducts that serve the city. But this is an unambitious piece of

A columbarium: a sepulchral chamber with niches and urns containing the ashes of the dead.

work, and its course is entirely underground until it reaches the inner city. The first of the above-ground aqueducts was the aqua Marcia, bringing in water on great arches from a source 23 miles away from Rome—but covering 57 miles in its circuitous course. This is the aqueduct that supplies the water for the Baths of Caracalla and of Diocletian—and this water is regarded as the finest of all. Seven of the aqueducts were built during the days of the free Republic. Of these the Marcia, constructed 144—140 B.C., is supreme. Of the four which the emperors added, only Claudius's two, the one that bears his own

Via Appia

The Aqueducts: where the combined waters of the Anio Novus and aqua Claudia are intersected by the Marcia. The via Latina runs parallel to the aqua Claudia and is connected by a crossroad to the via Appia in the distance.

name and the Anio Novus, deserve comparison with the Marcia. The Claudia is over 43 miles long, but some 34 miles lie underground. It is near the city, and particularly within the city, that its grandeur can best be appreciated. It is especially fine where it crosses the Caelian hill to take water to the Palatine, on the "Neronian arches". The Anio Novus takes its water from the river of that name. It is 54 miles long, of which again only some 9 miles are carried on arches above ground. For most of this distance the arches are those of the aqua Claudia, for the channel of the Anio Novus was laid

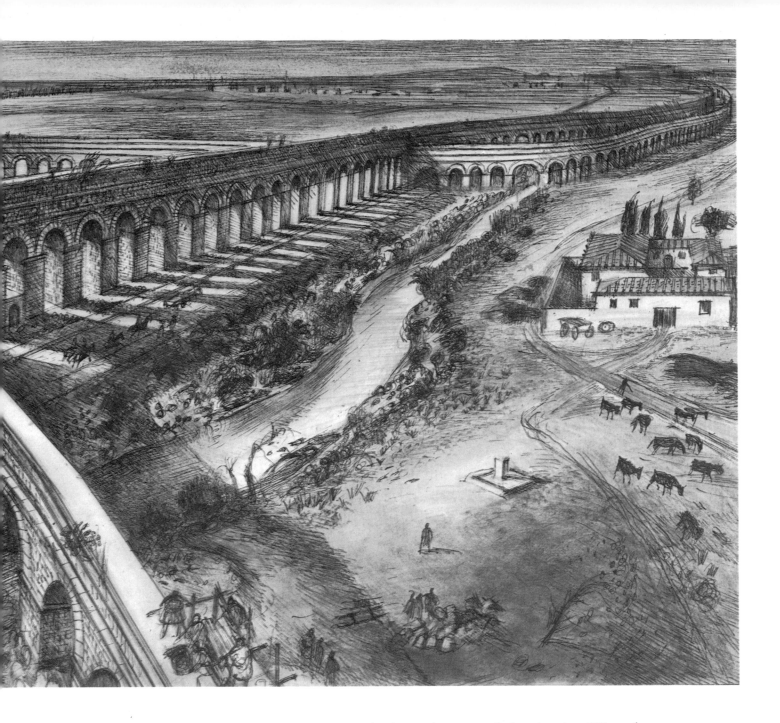

above the Claudia's channel. At one point, a little to the east of the Appian Way, the united channels of these two aqueducts and the aqua Marcia run close together, some 2½ miles beyond Aurelian's Wall, with the via Latina passing alongside. Here the Marcia makes a great loop, but the engineers of the Claudia directed their arches straight on, intersecting the Marcia at two points over 800 yards apart.

Once out in the countryside, it is worth taking the chance of a further excursion before going back to the city. The provincial to whom the name of Hadrian still means something may feel attracted to make a detour north-eastwards. Crossing the via Labicana and the via Praenestina, one joins the via Tiburtina going east from Rome up the valley

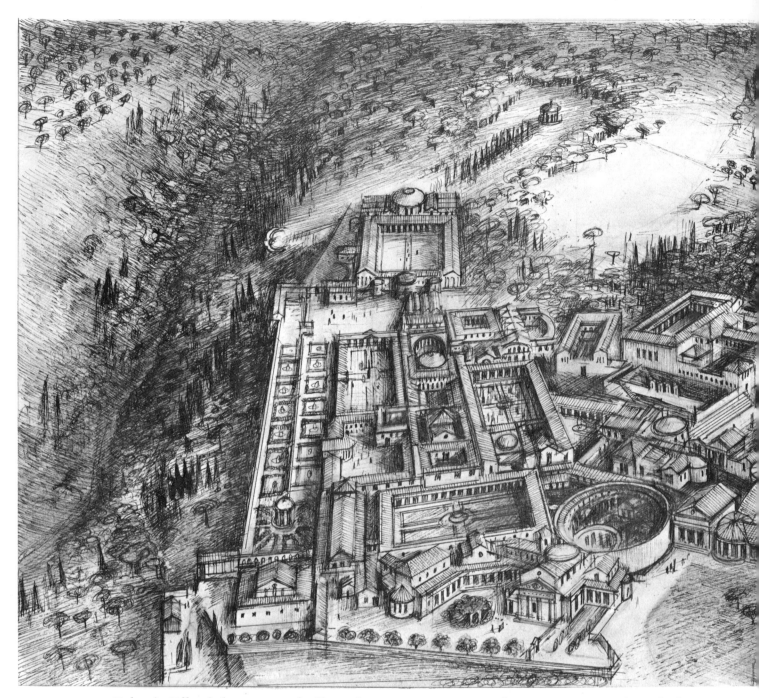

Hadrian's Villa, the largest imperial villa in the Roman Empire. It was begun in A.D. 125 and completed ten years later, and included reproductions of buildings which had most impressed the Emperor during his journeys abroad.

of the Anio, into the Sabine hills. Here, 20 miles from the capital, at Tibur, Hadrian built himself a country palace which may still be visited. This vast complex of halls, baths, theatres, lakes, porticoes, temples and ornamental gardens was Hadrian's pride and joy. It covers over 100 acres, with a circumference of several miles. Hadrian took a personal hand in its design, uninhibited by public necessities as he had been in Rome. Its parks and buildings are filled with originals or copies of works of art from all the

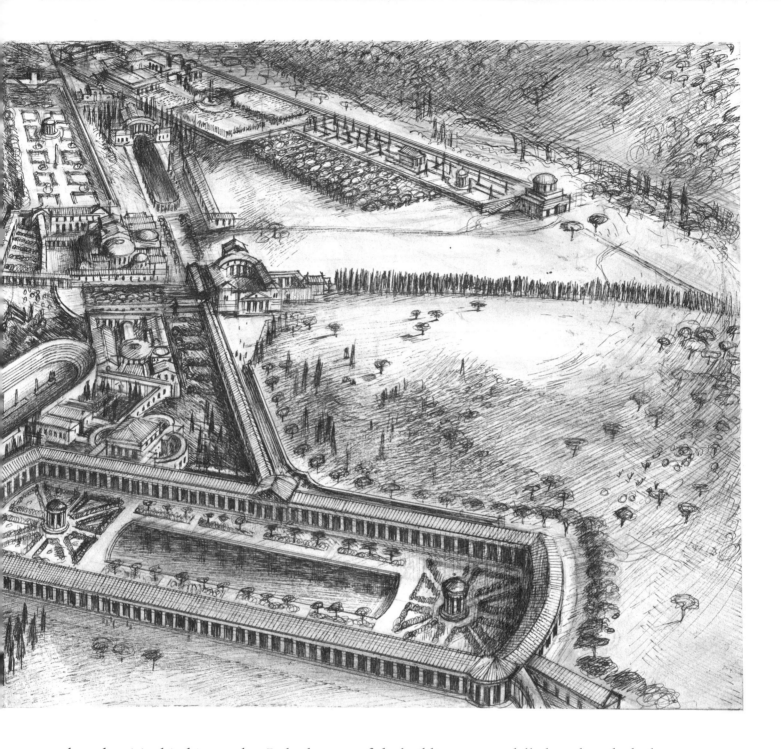

places he visited in his travels. Indeed, many of the buildings are modelled on those he had seen overseas, in Athens, Alexandria and elsewhere. The gardens are landscaped to recall scenes that attracted him when he was in Greece and Asia. Here the restless emperor, unpopular with the senate, who feared his energy and resented his neglect of them in favour of the provincials, could relax among mementoes of the people to whose welfare he devoted the twenty-one years of his reign.

Hadrian was born in Spain, of colonial descent. As a young man his "rustic accent" had caused him embarrassment. As emperor he symbolized the new relation between the city and the lands that had become Roman. Although his successor Antoninus reversed the trend and spent his entire reign, even longer than Hadrian's own, in Rome and the rest of Italy, that was a golden, Indian summer for the imperial city. The northern barbarians were beginning to become restive after a century and a half of peace on the frontiers. In A.D. 170 Italy herself was invaded by a foreign foe for the first time for nearly 300 years. The third-century emperors, faced with appalling difficulties, battled continuously with these northern enemies when other preoccupations permitted. From A.D. 212 all free inhabitants of the empire have been Roman citizens. The most remarkable contribution to restoring the balance in the north and giving Rome a further respite, has been made by emperors born in the rugged mountains between the Adriatic and the Danube. It is from here that Constantine's own family comes. Some instinct perhaps led him, as he travelled between Europe and Asia, to contemplate a new capital nearer his birthplace than Rome—and more strategically placed to resist external aggression. But even if the emperor has reduced the status of Rome, and perhaps weakened her by withdrawing resources which are now spent elsewhere, the future of the sacred and eternal city still seems assured. It was an early Christian writer—who had no love for Rome—who asked: "Was there ever a city like the Great City?"

Constantine the Great, from the fragment of a colossal statue at the Vatican.

BIBLIOGRAPHY

A. BOETHIUS   *The Golden House of Nero* (1961) (On private houses and apartment buildings)

D. R. DUDLEY   *Urbs Roma: a source-book of classical texts on the city and its monuments* (1967)

E. NASH   *A Pictorial Dictionary of Ancient Rome*, 2 vols (1961)

U. E. PAOLI   *Rome: its People, Life and Customs* (1963)

S. B. PLATNER and T. ASHBY   *A Topographical Dictionary of Ancient Rome* (1929)

M. R. SCHERER   *Marvels of Ancient Rome* (1955)

H. H. SCULLARD   *The Etruscan Cities and Rome* (1967)

E. M. WINSLOW   *A Libation to the Gods* (1963) (On the aqueducts)

ARTIST'S BIBLIOGRAPHY

S. B. PLATNER and T. ASHBY   *A Topographical Dictionary of Ancient Rome* (Oxford University Press)

ERNEST NASH   *Pictorial Dictionary of Ancient Rome* (Zwemmer)

H. STUART JONES   *Companion to Roman History* (Oxford University Press)

U. E. PAOLI   *Rome: its people, life and customs* (Longmans)

DONALD R. DUDLEY   *Urbs Roma* (Phaidon)

MICHAEL GRANT   *The Climax of Rome* (Weidenfeld & Nicolson)

GIULIO GIANNELLI   *The World of Ancient Rome* (Macdonald)

IAN A. RICHMOND   *The City Wall of Imperial Rome* (Oxford University Press)

THOMAS ASHBY   *The Aqueducts of Ancient Rome* (Oxford University Press)

MORTIMER WHEELER   *Roman Art and Architecture* (Thames and Hudson)
                             The Birth of Western Civilisation (Thames and Hudson)

BANISTER FLETCHER   *A History of Architecture* (Athlone Press)

INDEX

The references in italics refer to the drawings